SELF-IMAGE:
YOUR VISION OF WELLNESS

DR. ROBERT L. WILSON JR., DSL

Archway Publishing books may be ordered through booksellers or by contacting:

Archway Publishing
1663 Liberty Drive
Bloomington, IN 47403
www.archwaypublishing.com
844-669-3957

ISBN: 978-1-6657-3366-3 (sc)
ISBN: 978-1-6657-3367-0 (e)

Library of Congress Control Number: 2022921403

Print information available on the last page.

Archway Publishing rev. date: 01/05/2023

CONTENTS

PREFACE

My training, consulting, life and wellness coaching, hypnotherapy, leadership, education, and continuing-education experience, being a mindfulness and Neuro-Linguistic Programming Practitioner (NLP), along with my background working in the mental health field provides a robust conceptual and experiential lens to help bridge the gaps among the awareness, the process, and the practice of wellness in real life. As the owner of businesses and an online academy that focus on personal, professional, leadership, and organizational education, development, and training, I help facilitate change, development, transition, growth, and transformation from the inside out!

This is a guide to facilitate your journey of discovering, unlocking, and maximizing your potential to fulfill your purpose, create, and increase wellness for optimal success from the inside out! Wellness is a journey and not a destination. A big part of this journey is awakening to discover who you are, unlock your capabilities, and maximize your possibilities for success! Welcome to the journey of a lifetime!

This conversation is not about providing more information on wellness. It's about understanding wellness from a different perspective to bring you new awareness and assist you with applying that information in your life. This book introduces the idea of visualizing wellness as being created rather than achieved. This means that you have the power, control, and ability to create opportunities that will manifest your desired goals and outcomes of wellness.

This new dialogue will help raise your consciousness of the role and creative power that positive self-image has in creating optimal wellness and the behaviors that are programmed by that image. "What keeps people from doing what they know they need to do for themselves?" (Arloski, 2014, p. xv). This self-image and wellness book helps answer this question. Not knowing what to do seems most important externally, but the critical missing component is understanding how to create the self-image of your desired wellness goals from the inside out! What keeps people from doing what they know they should do is what and who they become.

I developed these concepts and wrote this book to assist you with gaining awareness, understanding, and application of the process for creating your self-image so you can more intentionally shift your wellness practices dimensionally and holistically. This book uses the eight dimensions of the wellness model to guide the discussion, digestion, and demonstration because the emphasis is that wellness is holistic. All the dimensions that work toward optimal well-being are interdependent. One dimension is not more important than another.

What makes this book unique compared with the typical self-help or wellness books is that it focuses on self-education, self-motivation, and self-empowerment to provide what we call *self-help*. Self-help comes from a self-awareness and self-determination perspective, empowering individuals to develop their internal resources so they can produce external results. It is critical to recognize your ability, choice, and power to change things for yourself. This is not a prescription telling you what to do or how to do it; rather, it brings you awareness of the information, application, and practice of creating wellness, which can intentionally and strategically shift your overall quality of life.

I discuss self-help from an internal ideal and bridge the gap to external outcomes. This involves helping you identify, create, or redefine your self-image of wellness to incorporate effective strategies for producing wellness holistically. It is important that you understand the relevance of the information being presented and how to implement it to help you effectively build wellness plans, strategies, and goals for successfully creating and maintaining a healthier lifestyle (Arloski, 2014, p. xvi). This book provides opportunities for self-reflection to aid you in digesting and demonstrating the information for true core transformation.

The focal point of creating wellness is to provide awareness, education, development, and training of the creation process and its components. I use the Self-Determination Theory, which focuses on motivation and personality, and the Transfer of Learning Theory, which is based on the idea that knowledge learned in one area can be applicable in and across multiple contexts, settings, scenarios, and situations. These theories help us better understand how individuals are motivated, which affects their determination and ultimately their success.

I am using the Self-Determination Theory and Transfer of Learning Theory in writing this book because they will help you become aware of and understand the importance of how self-determination and self-motivation transfer in your learning along your wellness journey. This book is a look inside. Many people want success but may not be aware of the barriers that are hindering them or affecting their motivation to succeed.

According to the Center for Self-Determination Theory's website, "The Self-Determination Theory represents a broad framework for the study of human motivation and personality" (https://selfdetermi-nationtheory.org). This theory is helpful with understanding internal and external motivators and how you can intentionally use them to holistically improve your wellness. This lays a good foundation for you to consider what wellness looks and sounds like and how you can apply and practice the information in your life until there is a real trans-formation. "People are centrally concerned with motivation—how to move themselves or others to act" (https://selfdeterminationtheory. org). This theory captures the essence of how motivation and individ-ual personalities are interconnected.

This book's emphasis is on increasing understanding of wellness to guide and promote a healthier self-image and create good feelings of wellness. The format provides user-friendly information that purpose-fully enhances awareness, which you can incorporate into real life prac-tices. I also want to dispel the myth that wellness is solely a physical dimension and to expand your perspective on wellness across multiple dimensions for a holistic view. This will help you better understand how the eight dimensions of wellness are interconnected. Spiritual wellness affects intellectual wellness affects emotional wellness affects financial wellness affects physical wellness affects social wellness affects occupational wellness affects environmental wellness. It is easier to understand the dimensions individually, but we must be reminded that all of them are working together simultaneously and continuously.

How you feel and see yourself has a major impact on your overall wellness and what wellness is for you. I desire to empower, enlighten, encourage, and educate people to expand their definition of wellness for themselves. Many think that being well means not being sick, but they are not experiencing optimal health and wellness. What is optimal health and wellness anyway? Typically, people focus on health but minimize or leave out the concept of wellness.

Here, I want to use the term *wellness* and describe it and its impact from the inside out. Optimal wellness is not based on a reaction to something or someone; it is an intentional, purpose-driven choice to incorporate a process to maximize wellness. What? There are no limits to your creation and experience of wellness. The possibilities of your wellness experience are endless. With your hands, what are you going to create?

Wellness is dimensional and should be discussed in that capacity. My talking about dimensions helps to better explain and broaden the view that multiple elements, components, or degrees make up the overall wellness of an individual. All eight dimensions work together for overall wellness; however, we break down wellness dimensionally to define what each dimension includes and to strategically target specific areas to improve our wellness along the journey. Many people focus on health, which is only one dimension: the physical dimension of wellness. Our definition will include the eight dimensions of the wellness model to help readers expand their understanding,

DR. ROBERT L. WILSON JR., DSL

awareness, and practice of more holistic wellness goals, strategies, plans, and overall lifestyles.

WELLNESS

I want to define what *wellness* is since it has many connotations. Wellness includes self-education and the motivation to intentionally create it—to take inspired action by learning how to think, not what to think. I ask you to consider how you think so that you can start to notice and become more aware of it. This will empower you to create optimal wellness. How you imagine yourself is an integral part of the process for creating optimal well-being.

Wellness is about using a dimensional perspective to gain a more holistic view of life. I want this book to be an easy read of vital information that allows you to see new facets of yourself—to extract and draw out the value that you already have inside, such as your creativity, resourcefulness, and wholeness (Arloski, 2014). This insight builds your resilience as well as intentionally improves your confidence and competence. You have the tools; you just need to know how to access and use them.

Wellness affects your overall quality of life. Many people's journeys of wellness are in response to illness. I want you to shift your perception from achieving optimal wellness to creating it. Optimal wellness is a choice to create and improve without limits by others, your situation, or your circumstance. The goal is to discuss wellness in such a way that it empowers, educates, and enlightens you so that you can intentionally improve your wellness and build resilience, awareness, and understanding.

How do you define *wellness*? There are many definitions for what wellness is and the components it includes. We must have a working definition for wellness in this context to better understand its application. The National Wellness Institute defines wellness as "a process of becoming aware of making choices toward a more successful existence" (https://nationalwellness.org). This definition best embodies the empowerment emphasis needed for our purposes.

Wellness is not something that is achieved; it is a process for individuals to become aware and intentionally make choices that lead them toward a more successful existence. This allows individuals to not blame their circumstances, situations, or others for their wellness results or lack of results for that matter. It empowers individuals to take control of their wellness and lives! This definition shows that wellness is a process and not a destination. Understanding how that process works starts with building our self-image. Focusing on the connection between how we define wellness and how we create a self-image will help determine our level of wellness, our behaviors that support that image, and ultimately the results we produce.

The eight dimensions of wellness are as follows.

1. **Spiritual wellness:** Spiritual fulfillment, purpose, meaning, or identity, not necessarily religion
2. **Intellectual wellness:** Use of your mental capabilities to create, expand, and think in healthy ways
3. **Emotional wellness:** The awareness and ability to positively shift emotions
4. **Financial wellness:** Financial literacy, awareness, and freedom
5. **Physical wellness:** Exercise or activity, health, nutrition, and fitness
6. **Social wellness:** Healthy, happy, fulfilling relationships and interactions
7. **Occupational wellness:** Fulfillment and purpose in work that brings skills, satisfaction, and empowerment
8. **Environmental wellness:** Physical and mental environments conducive to providing safety, support, and stimulation

For additional information on the eight dimensions of wellness, you can visit the SAMHSA (2016) website (https://store.samhsa.gov/product/What-You-Need-to-Know-About-National-Wellness-Week/sma16-4952). These definitions are provided as baselines for you to explore, study, and define what they look, feel, and sound like for your desired wellness.

The eight wellness dimensions will help us take into consideration the components of life that affect our overall health and well-being. The eight dimensions help us identify different aspects of our lives that we want to improve. Although we focus on the eight dimensions of wellness, and we talk about wellness dimensionally, it is a holistic approach to recognize how each dimension feeds into our overall wellness results.

What are the eight dimensions of wellness? Take about ten to fifteen minutes to describe them in your own words. This will help you start constructing your image within each of these dimensions. It is important to your self-education, development, and training to start thinking about what you want these different areas of wellness to look, feel, and sound like.

EIGHT DIMENSIONS OF WELLNESS

In this section, I want you to define each of the eight dimensions of wellness in your own words based on the definitions I provided you as points of reference.

1. **Spiritual**

2. **Intellectual**

3. **Emotional**

4. **Financial**

5. **Physical**

6. **Social**

7. **Occupational**

8. **Environmental**

INTRODUCTION

Self-Image: Your Vision of Wellness captures that wellness is a choice and people can be empowered, enlightened, educated, and encouraged. Raising your awareness of this process will allow you to capture the interpersonal and intrapersonal components needed to change effectively and navigate wellness strategically and purposefully. I want to emphasize the impact of your self-image because many are trying to change things on the outside without first changing things on the inside regarding wellness and results. I developed this book to provide you with insight and guidance on adopting a more holistic approach to increase your wellness and intentionally build resilience. Your resilience comes from building your inner resources, shifting your mindset, and taking responsibility for consciously making your own choices, which influence your behavior. You have the ability, resources, and power to change, create, and experience wellness at the highest level (Arloski, 2014, p. 69).

Your wellness starts from the internal image that you have developed knowingly or unknowingly, and it is reflected in your external image of wellness. What does that mean? How you visualize yourself on the inside will be reflected in what you become and see on the outside. Many people may be unaware that this picture is running the show. My goal is to help you identify your self-image in different areas or dimensions of wellness so you can intentionally create or recreate your desired level of wellness.

MINDSET VERSUS MIND-SHIFT

To renew your perception of wellness, you must understand what a mindset and a mind-shift are. This is important in any process where change is the focal point; people need to clearly and honestly assess where they are (how they see themselves, talk about themselves, and feel about themselves) and what they want to accomplish. You must look at yourself as a whole person, not just the behaviors you want to improve (Arloski, 2014). Many people talk about changing their mindsets, which are fixed, when they should be talking about or creating mind-shifts, which will move them from their current way of thinking to a new way of thinking or perceiving.

It is important to understand your mindset to get your mind working for and with you because your beliefs and your way of thinking influence your behavior (Gomas, 2017). A *mind-shift* means identifying those fixed beliefs that are no longer serving you and replacing them with new habits that you want—replacing those old beliefs with new beliefs that support the image and the results you want to create.

Wellness is a result of your mindset and the beliefs you have about the eight dimensions of wellness that represent different aspects of your life. Mind-shifts allow for new focuses and results that you create within the eight dimensions of wellness. These are governed by changing the position and placement of your perceptions—or in other words, repositioning the way that you see, feel, and think about things from the inside out.

Mindsets and mind-shifts both deal with your beliefs. Mindsets deal with past beliefs that you have already created, and mind-shifts focus on creating new beliefs. "Beliefs determine your behavior, not the other way around. A belief is a strongly held opinion about yourself or the world around you. Beliefs often create habitual patterns of thought that continue to play over and over in our hearts and minds" (Gomas, 2017). Your beliefs create your self-image, which influences how you behave.

You must identify your current mindset by first asking, "How do I see myself?" Take some time to reflect on this question; it doesn't have to be a quick answer. For the mind-shift to take place, you must start by changing the image that you want to have in a specific dimension of wellness. Ask yourself, "What do I want to see and be?" How will you feel when you see and become that person? Create a new image that reflects the desired outcome. As you reinforce this image, you will shift from your current mindset to a new mindset. In doing so, you will reprogram your behavior for your new desired outcome. You must take responsibility to change your perception of yourself. By changing or shifting your perception and beliefs about yourself, you will create the program for your new behaviors to follow (Arloski, 2014).

CHANGING YOUR MINDSET

Now that I've defined and explained mindset and mind-shift, I will discuss how you change your current fixed mindset. You must first notice and be aware of what your current mindset is. Your current mindset is producing your results or lack of results. A good way to identify your current mindset within the eight dimensions of wellness is to go through each dimension and write down what you currently see in each of those dimensions. What do you currently see or experience in the following areas: spiritual wellness, intellectual wellness, emotional wellness, financial wellness, physical wellness, social wellness, occupational wellness, and environmental wellness? Is it positive or negative? Is it effective or ineffective? That will be an indicator of your current mindset and reality.

For example, you might say, "regarding your occupational wellness, I don't like my job, I feel stuck, and I don't enjoy what I am doing. My perspective of work is a negative one and my mindset is too. I would like to have a different mindset regarding work. I would like to enjoy the work that I do. I want to make great money. I want to feel valued and fulfilled. I want to create this positive mindset and wellness." Now write down what you would like to see, how you would like to feel, and what you would like to hear in each of the eight dimensions. Take some time to identify your current mindset and the mind-shift you desire; recognizing your current way of thinking and deciding what you want your thinking and outcome to be may take time.

The mind-shift starts with a new desire. The next step is creating the self-image that you want to see. It is important to choose words that will start to create the desired outcomes that you want. For instance, you might say, "regarding your occupational wellness, I see myself doing work that is fun and exciting. I get paid very well and I am amazing at what I do. I am fulfilled and valued!" How will this make you feel? What positive emotions will accompany the things you just said? Are you grateful, happy, excited, et cetera? Now attach those positive emotions to the image that you described with your words to create it; consistently say those words and be very detailed about it. The more you can feel those positive emotions and see the image being your reality, the more your mind-shift will move away from the old mindset from the inside out. Remember that the outside reflects the inside.

WELLNESS TRANSFORMATION

Reflective Thoughts

Take a few minutes to reflect on the questions regarding your wellness and answer accordingly.

1. What have you learned?

2. What new awareness or insights do you have?

3. What do you see, feel, or hear because of this new awareness?

4. What is your current mindset? Notice what you think and how you think.

5. What is your mind-shift? Consider what you would like to think and how you would like to think.

6. What three things will you focus on doing now?

7. What are some challenges and opportunities of implementing the three things you will focus on doing now?

DR. ROBERT L. WILSON JR., DSL

SELF-IMAGE

Self-image will be the starting point for discussing and developing your mindset to promote a healthier wellness perspective. A powerful part of creating a healthy life vision is clearly detailing what wellness truly looks like for you (Arloski, 2014, p. 158). Your image—or more importantly, your self-image—will govern your view and practices of what wellness is for you. Self-image has a lot to do with wellness. We think in pictures. When I say dog, you don't think of the letters d-o-g but rather you think of a picture of a dog.

What is *self-image*? Self image is the picture you construct of yourself internally based on thoughts, experiences, and words that you use, or others have used toward you and you either accepted or agreed with. Your self-image influences how you see yourself and what wellness looks, feels, and sounds like to you. Self-image gives us a better grasp on the images that we associate with our overall wellness. Our wellness starts internally with the self-image that we have in those specific areas.

Your wellness is an external self-reflection of your self-image. It mirrors what is developed and believed inside; it embodies the self-image you have. Changing your behaviors to live a healthier life without changing the internal patterns will be difficult. Your self-image, or your internal picture of yourself, is connected to your identity and your belief system, and determines the behaviors that reinforce that image. Building a healthier lifestyle starts with how you view yourself and the process of creating a healthy life vision (Arloski, 2014, p. 157). The purpose of using self-image is to empower you to recognize both unhealthy and healthy images you may have associated with the different dimensions of wellness that you choose to create and improve.

Your self-image of wellness is based on several factors, such as your experiences, words, and background. Many people are not aware of their self-image or how redefining their self-image can help them achieve their desired outcomes. Self-image is important on the wellness journey because self-image is where wellness is created; it plays a critical role in optimal wellness. Wellness is both an external manifestation and an internal image that the individual has. I want to make the concept of self-image user friendly and comprehendible to assist you with effectively applying this information for transformation in your life.

SELF-IMAGE AND SELF-IDENTITY

It is important to discuss self-image and self-identity because the self-image that you have is based on how you see yourself and the beliefs that you develop around your identity, which create the behaviors that you manifest externally. Many are trying to make behavioral changes without changing the beliefs that support their identity, which the behaviors reinforce. With holistic wellness, it is critical that you understand the self-image and identity you picture internally, which are connected to the things you believe about yourself. Ultimately, your behavior will always coincide with the image that you have.

You cannot have one self-image and identity and a different set of behaviors that reinforce a different self-image. You will become empowered and gain control of your wellness by intentionally creating the self-image and the identity that you desire. By adding new beliefs and attitudes associated with that new self-image, you will allow yourself to reprogram your behavior and to fulfill and demonstrate your new image. Now let us talk about how to change your self-image.

HOW TO CHANGE YOUR SELF-IMAGE

Now that you know your self-image helps create your wellness, how do you intentionally change your image? Remember, we think in pictures. Your self-image is created through visualization, words, and feelings. You intentionally change your image by monitoring how and what you see regarding your self-image. Words, thoughts, and feelings reinforce your image.

An important factor in creating a self-image of wellness in any of the eight dimensions of wellness is detailing the image you would like to see reflected in your reality. For example, if I want to change how I view myself in my physical dimension of wellness, I could get a picture of what I would like to look like physically. I could also identify the type and size of clothes I would like to wear. I could describe the narrative or conversation of how I want to look, feel, and hear regarding this desired outcome. This will help me reconstruct my internal picture of my physical dimension of wellness and reprogram myself so that my external behaviors will align with this dimension of wellness.

The more you can create visual, auditory, and kinesthetic parts to the image, the more ingrained the image will become. This reprograms your image subconsciously, which controls habitual behavior. So, the more you can see it, hear it, and feel it, the more this image will be held in your imagination and will be impressed upon your subconscious. It will become real to you first on the inside, then on the outside.

This is important because the self-image programs behavior. Therefore, behavior is improved first by creating the image of the outcome you want, which guides your behavior or external outcomes. The more you can create a narrative that includes visuals, dialogues, affirmations, and positive feelings associated with your desires, the more you will be anchored to create the image of wellness that you desire.

SELF-IMAGE AND IMAGINATION

Self-image and imagination are connected because it's through your imagination that your self-image is constructed, changed, and developed. Imagination allows you to visualize this self-image or the pictures that you either desire or don't desire to have. Here, we want to discuss intentionally using our imagination to build the self-image of what we do want instead of what we don't want. Your self-image is created by visualizing an image repeatedly. It's very important to understand that the image you consistently give your attention to will manifest in your life. By using your imagination, you train yourself to picture what you want to do, be, and have. "Imagination is the beginning of creation" (Goddard, 1966, p. 39). The more you imagine it, add details to the image, and hold it in your mind, the more you direct your thoughts and desires to create that internal picture in your outward reality.

Using your imagination means seeing yourself having, being, or doing the thing you desire. Learning how to use your imagination to visualize wellness is the key to effective wellness creation and success. "Visualizing is the great secret of success" (Behrend, 2013, p. 14). To experience freedom, wellness, and happiness, you must deliberately control your imagination along with the feeling that accompanies it to form your desired image and degree of wellness (Goddard, 2020, p. 25). You must visualize, feel, and hear the things associated with this desire when completely fulfilled. You get a chance to play with the possibilities by imagining and by creating the pictures that you want to see in your reality. The secret to your wellness success is first seeing, feeling, and hearing what that success looks, feels, and sounds like through your imagination. Remember your thoughts become things and something must first be a thought before it can become a thing. That means what you're consistently thinking about, and visualizing will become real in your life. You choose intentionally or unintentionally.

SELF-IMAGE QUESTIONS

One of the best ways to change your image is to pose questions to yourself about yourself. Self-image questions allow for self-reflection and introspection about who you are from your core. Here are some questions to help you use your imagination to create the self-image you desire: *What is my identity? Who am I? How do I see myself?* Your core (self-identity) is based on not your roles but the very essence of who you are on the inside or, in some situations, who you have been told you are. The self-image questions help you think about who you are, who you want to be, where you are, where you want to go, what you're currently doing, and what you would like to do.

You are awesome and wonderfully created. Your mind is phenomenal. It is important to understand how you can specifically use six mental faculties to create the self-image you want. Those six mental faculties are your imagination, intuition, will, memory, reason, and perception. The questions allow for use of your imagination, intuition, will, memory, reason, and perception. These six mental faculties are activated and collaborate when you ask yourself the following questions to help you define and redefine, shape, and reshape, and create every picture of yourself that is represented in each of the eight dimensions of wellness. Ask yourself these self-image questions that call on you to ponder and reflect without giving a quick choreographed answer. The purpose of the self-image questions is to cause you to notice the image you have of yourself, the image you want to have of yourself, and the desire to shift from one to the other.

QUESTIONS TO GUIDE SELF-IMAGE CHANGE

Take thirty minutes to think about and answer the following self-image questions.

1. Who am I?
2. Who do I want to be?
3. What do I want to do?
4. What do I want to have?
5. What do I want to look like?
6. What types of relationships do I want to have?
7. How do I talk?
8. How do I walk?
9. How do I dress?
10. Who are my friends?
11. How do I talk about myself?
12. How do I want others to talk about me?
13. How do I want to feel?
14. How do I see myself?
15. What are my best qualities?
16. What do I love about myself?
17. Do I feel deserving and worthy?
18. What am I grateful for?
19. How do I celebrate myself?
20. What does the best version of me look, sound, and feel like?
21. What are the positive things that I want to hear about myself?

What did you notice or become aware of as you answered the questions?

SELF-IMAGE TRANSFORMATION

Reflective Thoughts

Take a few minutes to reflect on the questions regarding your self-image and answer accordingly.

1. What have you learned?

2. What new awareness or insights do you have?

3. What do you see, feel, or hear because of this new awareness?

4. What is your current mindset? Notice what you think and how you think.

5. What is your mind-shift? Consider what you would like to think and how you would like to think.

6. What three things will you focus on doing now?

7. What are some challenges and opportunities of implementing the three things you will focus on doing now?

SELF-DETERMINATION THEORY

Applying the Self-Determination Theory will help you understand your internal and external motivations for wellness. This will be instrumental in developing strategic goals, plans, and outcomes. Motivation is a determining factor in effectively building your self-image and positively shifting your feelings to improve your wellness. Therefore, the Self-Determination Theory will assist you with this process of understanding and implementing determination and motivation strategies for success.

"Self-Determination Theory (SDT) represents a broad framework for the study of human motivation and personality" (Center for Self-Determination Theory). The Self-Determination Theory is utilized in this work because it creates a great awareness of both internal and external motivation for individuals regarding wellness. It helps individuals become more aware of the things that motivate them and affect their determination level. The theory helps people recognize both internal and external motivational factors that either increase or decrease their determination to successfully complete their dreams or aspirations. This theory embodies the wellness journey by giving individuals power and control in this journey, as well as in discovering, unlocking, and maximizing their potential.

The Self-Determination Theory will help you take on self-responsibility, self-accountability, and self-empowerment. This theory helps you take away or minimize blame on others, circumstances, or external factors. A better understanding of not only the journey to wellness but also the journey through yourself to better self-understanding will help you more effectively reach your goals.

I will discuss how your internal and external motivation lead to your determined self-motivation. Your intrinsic motivation is what motivates you from within or internally influences your behavior. Examples are having a sense of pride, experiencing enjoyment, taking on a challenge, feeling good about yourself, doing the right thing, and upholding your values and standards, accomplishments, and progress toward a goal or outcome. Extrinsic motivation includes the external factors that influence your behavior. Examples are praise, weight loss, new wardrobe, new relationships, awards, certificates, more income, a better job, and a new home. The Self-Determination Theory is a broad framework or infrastructure to assist us with understanding factors that contribute to both determination and motivation for wellness (Ryan and Deci, 2020, p. 1).

According to the Center for Self-Determination Theory website, motivation is influenced based on "the distinctions between intrinsic and extrinsic goals and their impact on motivation and wellness." Your ability to set goals based on your motivation for well-being can affect your outcomes and results. Therefore, to be successful, you should set wellness goals based on the internal and external factors that motivate you. Instead of finding ways to motivate yourself to reach your goal, you should set your goal based on what already motivates you internally or externally.

This theory is used and explained because becoming aware of both your intrinsic and extrinsic motivators is important to better understand what motivates you and how. Knowledge of your self-image, its relatedness to your wellness dimensionality, and your autonomy (the ability to govern and choose what you want wellness to look, feel, or sound like) will determine your level of determination to make changes for improvement (Martela and Ryan, 2015, p. 2).

SELF-DETERMINATION THEORY

Take ten to fifteen minutes to write down what you think your internal and external motivators are. There are no right or wrong answers. The purpose of this activity is to start becoming consciously aware of what motivates you.

1.

2.

3.

4.

5.

6.

7.

8.

9.

10.

As a result, you can anchor both internal and external motivators in your life to help increase your determination and ability to succeed in your goals, desires, and outcomes. You can strategically implement what motivates you into a plan to reach your goals of wellness.

SELF-DETERMINATION THEORY TRANSFORMATION

Reflective Thoughts

Take a few minutes to reflect on the questions regarding self-determination theory and answer accordingly.

1. What have you learned?

2. What new awareness or insights do you have?

3. What do you see, feel, or hear because of this new awareness?

4. What is your current mindset? Notice what you think and how you think.

5. What is your mind-shift? Consider what you would like to think and how you would like to think.

6. What three things will you focus on doing now?

7. What are some challenges and opportunities of implementing the three things you will focus on doing now?

SELF-AWARENESS AND SELF-DETERMINATION

Self-awareness and self-determination greatly affect your level of wellness. Together, self-awareness and self-determination equal self-education. Self-empowerment comes from being educated about who you are. Much of the work for wellness is internal, not external. This does not mean that you don't have to do things externally to reach your wellness goals. What this does mean is that without laying the internal foundation first, all the things you do externally will not be as effective or have long-lasting results.

Self-awareness, self-determination, and self-empowerment are most of the work to create the wellness you desire. These are how you create the desired self-image and create the good feelings associated with that image. Therefore, programming yourself internally will display the behaviors that support the image you have now created.

Both awareness and determination are self-governed, which affects wellness choices and the process that engages you on your wellness journey. You have the power of choice! Understanding self-determination can help you become more conscious and directed in enhancing your motivation to reach your wellness goals. It is important to raise your awareness of what wellness is and how you see challenges or opportunities to improve. Your determination will work in conjunction with your awareness of information and how to apply that information to your individual wellness goals and plan.

Self-awareness is your ability to intentionally recognize various aspects of the eight dimensions that contribute to your wellness. *Self-determination* is your ability to intentionally focus on and allow change

DR. ROBERT L. WILSON JR., DSL

of the factors that contribute to your wellness choices. Focus and allow change to happen; do not force it. Your wellness behaviors reflect your level of self-awareness and self-determination connected to your self-image. Consciousness embodies awareness and determination for things to work by purposefully focusing your attention and shifting your perceptions to ensure your success (Arloski, 2014, pp. 98–99).

Self-awareness and self-determination are key ingredients to help you create strategies, goals, and plans that reflect your willingness and capacity for change. Self-awareness is about gaining insight into and understanding of where you are and where you want to go. Self-determination is about your ability to stay focused and determined to intentionally reach a goal, desire, or accomplishment. Goal setting is not about being told what to do; it's about tapping into your readiness for change using Prochaska's model (stages of change), goals, desires, and supports (Arloski, 2014, pp. 166–167).

SELF-AWARENESS AND SELF-DETERMINATION TRANSFORMATION

Reflective Thoughts

Take a few minutes to reflect on the questions regarding your self-awareness and self-determination and answer accordingly.

1. What have you learned?

2. What new awareness or insights do you have?

3. What do you see, feel, or hear because of this new awareness?

4. What is your current mindset? Notice what you think and how you think.

5. What is your mind-shift? Consider what you would like to think and how you would like to think.

6. What three things will you focus on doing now?

7. What are some challenges and opportunities of implementing the three things you will focus on doing now?

DR. ROBERT L. WILSON JR., DSL

TRANSFER OF LEARNING THEORY

Awareness of how you learn and how to transfer what you have learned will better undergird your determination and motivation to reach your desired level of wellness and success. An important part of knowledge is transferring what you've learned to practice. In this section, I will discuss the Transfer of Learning Theory. The Transfer of Learning Theory is based on the idea that knowledge learned in one area can be applicable across multiple contexts, settings, scenarios, and situations. This theory helps with guiding the self-education process because the purpose of this information is to ensure that you as the reader can apply or transfer the acquired knowledge in this book in various ways and under different circumstances (Hajian, 2019, p. 94).

Why is the transfer of learning important? You define a big part of your self-image of wellness through studying and discovering yourself. How does that study in discovery transfer to what you have learned or are learning? The only way to gain knowledge of your self-image, wellness, and motivation and the creative process is through studying, as well as intelligently organizing and directing the knowledge you're gaining through this book into practice (Proctor, 2021, p. 129). However, not all knowledge gets transferred into effective learning. To help combat the ineffectiveness of learning transfer, you can add elements that include reflection, application, skill, and self-education (Hajian, 2019, p. 99). All these elements are included in this book to assist you with transferring what you learn from what you read to your actual practices thereafter.

STUDY AND PRACTICE

"The only way to develop understanding is through study" (Proctor, 2021, p. 129). Awareness should lead to study, which produces greater understanding, which guides better application of the content and transforms your life practices. The self-education component needed for true change means not studying the information for studying's sake but studying yourself and how the information specifically raises your awareness and increases your understanding. Effectively demonstrating application can produce practices that foster greater wellness results for you.

You must develop the habit of repeating this information to expand your thinking and belief system and to support the desired wellness images that you are creating within the eight dimensions (Proctor, 2021, p. 129). Through studying this material, you are learning, unlearning, and relearning how to build your self-image. And you are learning how to connect your positive emotions as you program and reprogram the paradigm that will produce the behavior and the external results that you strategically want.

SELF-IMAGE, FEELINGS, AND BEHAVIOR

Self-image, feelings, and behavior play integral roles in the wellness journey. What are the connections between your self-image, feelings, and behavior? It is important to understand how your self-image connects to what you see and feel, and the behaviors that reflect what you see and feel. Seeing and feeling are internal, and behavior is the external reflection of what has been programmed internally. Your self-image (or what you see and how you feel) programs your behavior. Think about the dimension of wellness you choose to change and why. What do you see, how do you feel, and how will you behave in your new desired self-image of that dimension of wellness?

Your self-image and how you feel affect how you behave. The picture that you have of wellness and your feelings around wellness will influence your habitual behavior, and that behavior reinforces either a positive wellness image or a negative wellness image. I want to help connect the dots for you to understand how these three elements play major roles in the accomplishment of optimal wellness.

Wellness is about the self-image that you see, how you feel about that self-image in that specific dimension, and your behavior that will support the image and feeling of that wellness. In any wellness process for a change, it is important to assess how you see yourself and how you feel in the wellness dimension that you are creating a plan for. A part of the process is setting the focus of the foundational work on self-image, feelings, and behavioral connection (Arloski, 2014, pp. 84–85).

SELF-IMAGE, FEELINGS, AND BEHAVIOR TRANSFORMATION

Reflective Thoughts

Take a few minutes to reflect on the questions regarding your self-image, feelings, and behavior transformation and answer accordingly.

1. What have you learned?

2. What new awareness or insights do you have?

3. What do you see, feel, or hear because of this new awareness?

4. What is your current mindset? Notice what you think and how you think.

5. What is your mind-shift? Consider what you would like to think and how you would like to think.

6. What three things will you focus on doing now?

7. What are some challenges and opportunities of implementing the three things you will focus on doing now?

DR. ROBERT L. WILSON JR., DSL

PARADIGMS, PROCESSES, AND PRACTICES

In this section, I will focus on how paradigms, processes, and practices are interconnected and how they collaborate in creating one's
self-image of wellness and results. The paradigm is the image that
an individual creates internally as a default that results in behaviors
and practices externally. The purpose of paradigms, processes, and
practices is to raise awareness that we all have paradigms, but many
are unaware of the process that leads to their practices or behaviors
in their lives.

The paradigm of self-image governs the process that creates your
wellness outcomes and behavior practices. You can gain control over
the process of creating wellness by understanding what your current
paradigm is and changing that through the process of recreating
the current one as a new paradigm or desired self-image, which
will reprogram your wellness from the inside out. This will lead to
different behaviors and practices that reinforce the desired wellness
paradigm or self-image. How does this work? The new self-image or
paradigm is reinforced by developing a belief system that supports
the new image and is expressed in behavior practices that become
habitual by default.

For example, say I want to be fit and healthy. The old image was of
being out of shape. I create a new paradigm by deciding that my new
image is of being fit. I cut out pictures of how I want to look. I write
out affirmations or positive statements that I will start speaking daily.
I think about how this new image of me looks and feels and what he
does. I attach positive feelings, like I feel excited, happy, thankful, et
cetera. Now, I see my image differently. I take control over the image
by attaching positive feelings to it. In the process, I change my beliefs,
and now, my actions or behavior practices start to reflect the image,
and my outcomes will be different based on the paradigm and process

that I have implemented. The outcomes can include losing weight, working out, and eating differently because they are reflective of the new image or paradigm.

In creating a new image of wellness in any of the eight dimensions, you must strategically define and shape your self-image or paradigm to what you desire. You can do this by developing a new belief system that supports the new image of what you want (shifting from what you currently believe to what you want to believe and why).

REFLECTIVE JOURNAL

Additional Thoughts, Feelings, or Words to Share

Here, you can share any additional thoughts, feelings, or words based on the book.

EIGHT DIMENSIONS OF WELLNESS

What self-image would you like to create for the eight dimensions of wellness? What does it look, sound, and feel like for you?

1. Spiritual wellness
2. Intellectual wellness
3. Emotional wellness
4. Financial wellness
5. Physical wellness
6. Social wellness
7. Occupational wellness
8. Environmental wellness

SPIRITUAL WELLNESS

What do you want to be, do, and have?

INTELLECTUAL WELLNESS

What do you want to be, do, and have?

DR. ROBERT L. WILSON JR., DSL

EMOTIONAL WELLNESS

What do you want to be, do, and have?

FINANCIAL WELLNESS

What do you want to be, do, and have?

PHYSICAL WELLNESS

What do you want to be, do, and have

SOCIAL WELLNESS

What do you want to be, do, and have?

OCCUPATIONAL WELLNESS

What do you want to be, do, and have?

ENVIRONMENTAL WELLNESS

What do you want to be, do, and have?

DR. ROBERT L. WILSON JR., DSL

STRATEGIC PLAN

A strategic plan is necessary to successfully implement the information provided in this book. You need several elements to create a strategic plan. One way to create a strategic plan is to create SMART goals. The acronym SMART (specific, measurable, achievable, relevant, and time bound) helps you tailor your goals intentionally.

SMART goals address a timeline. Please use the following SMART goals activity to create a strategic plan for developing your new self-image in each of the eight dimensions of wellness and for creating your desired wellness goals and outcomes.

SMART GOALS

1. **Specific:** What are you going to be? What are you going to do? What are you going to have?

2. **Measurable:** How will you measure this goal? How will you know when you have achieved your goal?

3. **Achievable:** Is your goal realistic? Doable?

4. **Relevant:** Does your goal fit what you really want?

5. **Time bound:** When will this happen for you?

DAILY PRACTICE

Answering the following questions can help you think about and implement daily practices to facilitate your wellness goals.

1. What will you do in your daily practice?

2. What will you be thinking, visualizing, hearing, and feeling daily?

3. How will you act and feel once your wellness goal is accomplished?

CONCLUSION

This book focuses on both the awareness and the practice of increasing wellness from the inside out using self-education and self-study. The study is in the form of what enhances your determination as you transfer your learning into real results and positive outcomes. This information can change both your internal dialogue and the conversations that you have about what wellness is, what it looks like, what it sounds like, how to accomplish it, and how to enrich your experience! The self-image of wellness is a game changer because it changes how people think about wellness both dimensionally and holistically. It also shifts responsibility from outward factors to inward ownership, giving you the control and power of choice to create wellness instead of achieving it. You take control of your self-image through your imagination and build the life you want!

What a feeling of refreshment, empowerment, awareness, and education of a holistic view of wellness! This is an agent of transformation for those on their wellness journeys. By understanding your mindset and transitioning to your mind-shift, you create a path to successfully start the creation process. The information of the creation process will not only inform you but also help you transform your life. It's very important that you decide what you want to be, do, and have within each of the eight dimensions of wellness. This concept extracts information and adds value to how it can be practiced in helping individuals reach their wellness goals and dreams. The self-image of wellness approach helps you intentionally create optimal dimensional wellness by raising your awareness and increasing your understanding of the concept and how it can increase your confidence and competence in applying wellness strategies and practices.

Your reflection, motivation, and determination in using this information and taking inspired action by using a strategic plan that includes

SMART goals can help guide you in this process of wellness creation. Your daily practices will help you define and identify the thoughts and feelings that will reinforce the inner image so you can reproduce it in your outward reality and overall wellness. Much success on your wellness journey!

REFERENCES

Arloski, Michael. 2014. *Wellness Coaching for Lasting Lifestyle Change.* 2nd ed. Duluth, MN: Whole Person Associates, Inc.

Behrend, Genevieve. 2013. *Your Invisible Power.* Columbia, SC: Watchmaker Publishing.

Goddard, Neville. 1966. *Resurrection.* Camarillo, CA: DeVorss Publications.

Goddard, Neville. 2020. *The Power of Awareness: Unlocking the Law of Attraction.* Deluxe ed. Middletown, DE: G&D Media.

Gomas, Dennis C. 2017. *Christian Life Coaching: Bible.* Author.

Hajian, Shiva. 2019. "Transfer of Learning and Teaching: A Review of Transfer Theories and Effective Instructional Practices." *IAFOR Journal of Education* 7, no. 1: 93–111.

Martela, Frank, and Richard M. Ryan. 2015. The Benefits of Benevolence: Basic Psychological Needs, Beneficence, and the Enhancement of Well-Being. *Journal of Personality* 84, no. 6: 1–15.

Proctor, Bob. 2021. *Change Your Paradigm, Change Your Life: Flip That Switch Now!* Middletown, DE: G&D Media.

Ryan, Richard M., and Edward L. Deci. 2020. Intrinsic and Extrinsic Motivation from a Self-Determination Theory Perspective: Definitions, Theory, Practices, and Future Directions. *Contemporary Educational Psychology* 61, article 101860.

SAMHSA. 2016. *SAMHSA's Wellness Initiative: Wellness Community* (slide presentation). Accessed August 30, 2022. https://store.samhsa.gov/product/SAMHSA-s-Wellness-Initiative-Wellness-Community-Power-Point-Presentation/sma16-4955

ABOUT THE AUTHOR

Dr. Robert L. Wilson Jr., DSL is an author, entrepreneur, consultant, speaker, coach, and trainer. He holds a doctorate in strategic leadership, a master's in sociology, and a bachelor's in psychology. He is also a Certified Professional Life Coach, Certified Wellness Coach, Certified Life Coach, Certified Mindfulness Practitioner, Certified Neuro-Linguistic Programming Practitioner (NLP), and Certified Hypnotherapist.

Dr. Wilson is the owner and principal consultant of Robert Wilson Consulting and Wilson Global Outreach Solutions, as well as, the founder and lead trainer of Global Solutions Education and Training Academy. He has worked in the field of mental health, leadership, and organizational development for over twenty years. Dr. Wilson also has a rich background in building and facilitating learning action networking communities. His areas of focus are personal, professional, leadership, and organizational education, development, and training. He is a National Trainer and certified Mental Health First Aid Instructor for the adult and youth curriculum.

For additional information about services, products, or programs, please reach out to Dr. Wilson via the following contact information.

Dr. Robert L. Wilson Jr., DSL, CPLC, CWC
Owner and Principal Consultant
Robert Wilson Consulting
Wilson Global Outreach Solutions, LLC
www.WilsonGOS.com
Robert@WilsonGOS.com
Global Solutions Education and Training Academy
https://globalsolutionseducationandtrainingacademy.learnworlds.com

Printed in the United States
by Baker & Taylor Publisher Services